the FRAY

ISBN 978-1-4234-7858-4

HAL•LEONARD®
CORPORATION
7777 W. BLUEMOUND RD. P.O. BOX 13819 MILWAUKEE, WI 53213

In Australia Contact:
Hal Leonard Australia Pty. Ltd.
4 Lentara Court
Cheltenham, Victoria, 3192 Australia
Email: ausadmin@halleonard.com.au

Visit Hal Leonard Online at
www.halleonard.com

CONTENTS

SYNDICATE

Words and Music by JOSEPH KING,
ISAAC SLADE and DAVID WELSH

Moderately, with a half-time feel

ABSOLUTE

Words and Music by JOSEPH KING,
ISAAC SLADE and DAVID WELSH

Moderate Rock

YOU FOUND ME

Words and Music by JOSEPH KING
and ISAAC SLADE

* Recorded a half step lower.

SAY WHEN

Words and Music by JOSEPH KING,
ISAAC SLADE, DAVID WELSH
and BEN WYSOCKI

May-be God can be ___ on both ___ sides ___ of the gun. ___ Nev-er un-

Bm
D
Say when, and my own
Bm
F♯m
D
two hands will com - fort you
A
F♯m
E
to - night, to - night. Say when,
D
Bm
and my own two arms

NEVER SAY NEVER

Words and Music by JOSEPH KING,
ISAAC SLADE and DAVID WELSH

WHERE THE STORY ENDS

Words and Music by JOSEPH KING
and ISAAC SLADE

*Recorded a half step lower.

ENOUGH FOR NOW

Words and Music by JOSEPH KING
and ISAAC SLADE

* Recorded a half step lower.

G Em D Csus2
- row, he got five or six of bliss.
Em Csus2 G Em D
Left my moth - er's moth - er with - out so much as a
Csus2 Em D/F♯ G
kiss,
Csus2 D Em Csus2
as a kiss.
3fr

UNGODLY HOUR

Words and Music by JOSEPH KING
and ISAAC SLADE

Moderately, with a light feel

Don't ___ talk, ___ don't ___ say ___ a thing, ___ 'cause your
I ___ know ___ you're ___ leav - in' now, ___ 'cause I

eyes, they tell ___ me more ___ than your ___ words. ___
held on to ___ my way ___ tight - ly. ___

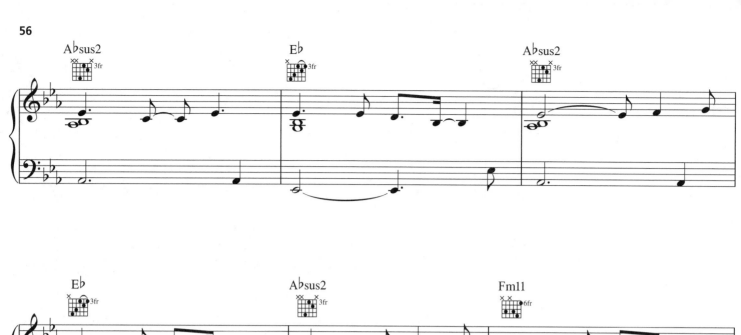

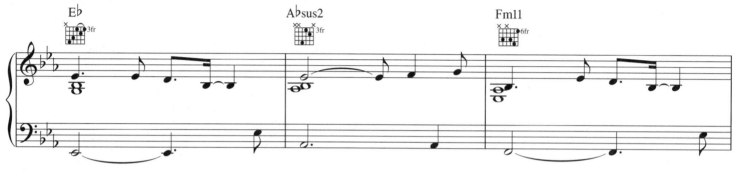

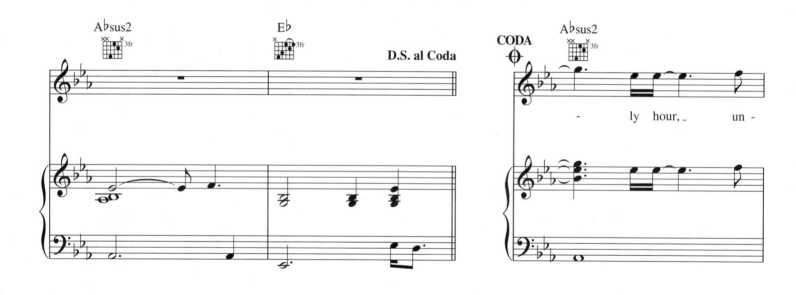

ly hour, _ un -

god - ly hour, _ un - god - ly hour. _ Her _ bag is now _ much

WE BUILD THEN WE BREAK

Words and Music by JOSEPH KING,
ISAAC SLADE, DAVID WELSH
and BEN WYSOCKI

Recorded a half step lower.

To Coda

HAPPINESS

Words and Music by JOSEPH KING,
ISAAC SLADE, DAVID WELSH
and BEN WYSOCKI

Moderately, with feeling